SACRED PATHWAYS

NINE WAYS TO CONNECT WITH GOD

STUDY GUIDE | FIVE SESSIONS

GARY THOMAS

WITH KEVIN AND SHERRY HARNEY

ZONDERVAN
Sacred Pathways Study Guide

Copyright © 2021 by Gary Thomas

This title is also available as a Zondervan ebook.

Requests for information should be addressed to: Zondervan, 3900 Sparks Dr. SE, Grand Rapids, Michigan 49546

ISBN 978-0-310-12209-8 (softcover)
ISBN 978-0-310-12210-4 (ebook)

All Scripture quotations are from The Holy Bible, New International Version®, NIV®. Copyright © 1973, 1978, 1984, 2011 by Biblica, Inc.® Used by permission. All rights reserved worldwide.

Any Internet addresses (websites, blogs, etc.) and telephone numbers in this book are offered as a resource. They are not intended in any way to be or imply an endorsement by Zondervan, nor does Zondervan vouch for the content of these sites and numbers for the life of this book.

First Printing February 2021 / Printed in the United States of America

CONTENTS

INTRODUCTION

THE LONGING OF THE SOUL

We are designed to connect with our God. There is something deep in every human being, even those who don't recognize it, that longs to know their Creator and the lover of their soul.

The One who formed us in our mother's womb and knew us before we breathed the air of this world is eternally relational. God exists in perpetual community as Father, Son, and Holy Spirit. Yet he still desires to be close to his children. He delights to be in relationship with us.

We feel this. We sense there is a part of us that hungers and thirsts for intimacy with our Maker. And when we get a taste of God's presence, we hunger for more. When God draws near us, we find ourselves looking for time and space to be with the One who cherishes us.

But here is the dilemma. Religious professionals seek to show us how to relate to our Creator. Faithful pastors, Sunday school teachers, and church leaders design a pathway for discipleship that they believe every Christian can walk. These individuals are well-meaning and kind, but they forget that a one-size-all approach almost never-fits-all. There is not one plan for discipleship. There is not a single pathway that *every* person should walk.

Have you ever met a parent who said, with a baffled look in his or her eyes, "I don't know what happened . . . I raised all my kids the same, but they turned out so different"? We know that every child is unique. God makes each one delightfully different. Ask the parents of identical twins or triplets if their kids are truly identical. These parents will tell you that, aside from their physical appearance, each one has their own passions, dreams, and approach to life.

When parents or teachers seek to press all children into the same mold, it always fails. Some are compliant by nature, others are adventurous, and some are outspoken. The only way to help children flourish is to unleash who *God* has designed them to be. If they are pressed into the same mold of learning, friendship, and play, there will be battles ahead.

The same is true for us. God has designed us with beautiful and diverse tastes in clothes, foods, interests, learning styles, and so much more. When we recognize this, we quickly realize that our pathway to intimacy with God will also be distinctive. If we ignore this fact and try to follow the path that someone else has set for us, we do a disservice to how God has made us. We will ultimately find ourselves spiritually frustrated, demotivated, or even bitter.

When we come to faith in Jesus, our unique personality, tastes, and outlook on life do not get erased. As a matter of fact, becoming a follower of Jesus should encourage us to pursue our God-given distinctives. Knowing that we are made by God and loved by him should give us peace with the things that make us who he wants us to be.

With this in mind, brace yourself for an amazing journey through *Sacred Pathways*. I think that you will find exciting new ways of connecting with God. You will understand others better and learn to celebrate the beautiful ways they meet with God. And you will encounter your Savior in new ways that will grow your intimacy with the One who loves you most.

Let the journey begin!

OF NOTE

The quotations interspersed throughout this study guide are excerpts from the book *Sacred Pathways: Nine Ways to Connect with God* and the video curriculum of the same name by Gary Thomas. All other resources, including the study introduction, small group questions, session introductions, prayer direction, and between-sessions materials have been written by Kevin and Sherry Harney in collaboration with Gary Thomas.

THE JOURNEY OF THE SOUL

Introduction to the Pathways

A journey with no direction, map, or pathway is a recipe for getting lost. That same journey—with pathways that fit our unique personality, style, and passions—is an exciting adventure!

INTRODUCTION

Daniel is fourteen. He grew up in the church and made the decision to receive God's grace through faith in Jesus. He loves sports, is outgoing, and gets excited by almost any challenge that comes his way. He loves fun and adventure and looks for ways to engage with people any time he can. *How would you guide Daniel in this critical season of his spiritual development?*

Tanya is twenty-three. She was raised in an atheistic home and never went to church. But now, due to the love and care of a college friend, she has placed her faith in Jesus. She is quiet. spends a lot of her time alone, and feels energized through solitude and silence. *What would you recommend Tanya do to take steps forward in knowing and loving Jesus?*

Manuel is thirty-five. He grew up in a Catholic home and always enjoyed going to Mass. He always felt connected to God through the rhythm and familiar words, songs, and smells that he experienced there. In his youth he walked away from the church, but now he finds himself wanting to connect with God again. He wonders how he can turn his heart back to God and recapture that sense of intimacy he felt as a young man. *What direction would you give him?*

Barbara is seventy-four. She has walked with Jesus for as long as she can remember. She still serves people in her community and church on a regular basis. She is part of a number of community groups for social connection, but she also has a passion to make the world a better place and help people in need. Her faith is real, but it seems to have gone flat and become routine. Barbara feels her passion is waning. *What might help ignite Barbara's faith in this season of life and give her fresh new vistas of engagement with God?*

It is unlikely that Daniel's pathway will look like Barbara's. Tanya's needs and temperament will certainly guide her to a different journey of faith than Manuel's. All these individuals are all seeking to move toward the same God, led by the same Holy Spirit, as they walk with the one Savior. Each is following a longing to be closer to God. But each one needs a unique and custom-made pathway that fits how God has made them.

Praise God that he has not limited his followers to only one pathway of spiritual growth and connection! The creative God who made each of us has offered many pathways to us that are clearly modeled in the Bible. We get the joy of discovering which pathways resonate for us and which pathways most naturally draw us closer to our Savior.

We were created to find our highest and truest and most intense delight in God.

TAKE THE ASSESSMENT

If you or any of your group members are just getting to know one another, take a few minutes to introduce yourselves. Then, to kick things off, take the personal assessment found in the back of this study guide. This assessment will give you a general idea of the particular pathway (or pathways) to which you gravitate. As you and your group members go through this study, you will learn more about each of these particular pathways to encountering God.

TALK ABOUT IT

Once everyone has completed the assessment, discuss one of the following questions:

- How were you taught to meet with Jesus? What methods, practices, and attitudes were taught to you as a young or new Christian?

— or —

- Choose one of the people in the session introduction. How might you encourage that person to move forward on his or her journey with God?

When someone really matters to us, we will count the cost and do anything to make sure we connect with that person!

TEACHING NOTES

As you watch the video for this session, use the following outline to record any thoughts or concepts that stand out to you.

Quincy . . . the newest member of the family

Hungering and thirsting for God

A wrong view of our time with God

What would you sacrifice to be with someone you truly love?

The danger of a one-size-fits-all approach to God

God made each one of us beautifully unique

Biblical examples of various spiritual pathways

The importance of desire

The best invitation you will ever receive

*If you are in a spiritual malaise, it may be
that you need a change in your spiritual diet.*

GROUP DISCUSSION

Take a few minutes with your group members to discuss what you just watched and explore these concepts in Scripture.

1. Describe a time in your journey of faith when you hungered for God more than anything else—even your own desires and dreams.

2. **Read Psalm 63:1–5.** Describe the heart and longing of David in this psalm. What do you think caused this level of hunger for God?

3. Why do you think Christians often refer to making time to be near God as a "discipline"? Why do we need effort to do something that should be a natural longing of our soul?

4. Tell about a time you changed your schedule, counted the cost, or shifted your plans to meet with someone who mattered to you. Why were you so willing to do this? How should this kind of thinking impact your desire to be with God?

5. What are some dangers of a "one-size-fits-all" approach to spending time with Jesus? Why is it so important to find ways to connect with your Savior that fit the way in which he has uniquely made you?

6. Tell about a person you know who meets with God in ways that are different from you. What have you learned from the example of this person?

7. When you think about the **pathways of wonder** (*naturalists, sensates,* and *traditionalists*), how can you see one of these fitting the way in which God has made you? What causes you to be in awe and wonder of God?

8. When you think about the **pathways of contemplation** (*enthusiasts, contemplatives,* and *intellectuals*), how might one of these help you draw near to God? How have you encountered God through your heart and mind?

9. When you think about the **pathways of action** (*ascetics, activists,* and *caregivers*), how can you see these helping you draw near your Creator? When was a time you engaged in an action that really connected you to the heart of God?

10. What are some of the dangers of not finding rich and meaningful ways to connect with God? What are some potential exciting new things that could happen if you engage in fresh new ways of drawing near to God and growing your relationship with him?

Delight is as powerful as discipline!

CLOSING PRAYER

Spend time as your group comes to a close to pray in some of the following directions:

- Thank God for the unique and beautiful way he has made each person in your small group.

- Give God praise for his amazing plan to create a wonderful array of pathways so that you can find joyful and fruitful ways to draw near to him.

- Ask the Holy Spirit to guide you over the coming sessions as you seek to discover new and dynamic ways to connect with the God who loves you.

- If you have taken the assessment and have a sense of your particular pathway, thank God for his leading and invite him to take you to even deeper places of intimacy with him.

The focus on spiritual temperaments is an attempt to help us understand how we best relate to God so we can develop new ways of drawing near to him.

BETWEEN-SESSIONS PERSONAL STUDY

Reflect on the content you've covered this week in *Sacred Pathways* by engaging in any or all of the following between-sessions activities. (This week, before you begin, you may want to review chapters 1–2 in the book.) The time you invest will be well spent, so let God use it to draw you closer to him. At your next meeting, share with your group any key points or insights that stood out to you as you spent this time with the Lord.

WHAT DO I LOVE TO DO?

What are three things you really enjoy doing?

Think about how you feel when you do these things. What expressions are on your face when you engage in them? How do you order your schedule so you can engage in them?

Take time to pray that you will grow to feel this same excitement, anticipation, and joy when you spend time with God.

A TIME OF REFLECTION

When do you tend to feel God's presence most powerfully?

What actions or experiences connect you closely to God?

What kind of places help you to notice and better tune into God's presence?

THE QUINCY CHALLENGE

Think back to the story of Quincy, the cavalier King Charles puppy, that you heard in this week's teaching. Take time today to watch a puppy or recall a past experience with a puppy or grown dog (since all dogs, at any age, still have a bit of a puppy in them). Take note of their loyalty, their devotion, and their focus on the approval of their owner.

What are three or four things that you learn about love and devotion from a puppy?

As you reflect on these lessons, what are a few ways that you can grow in devotion to and passion for the God who made you and loves to be with you?

LEARNING FROM THE MASTER

If you look closely at the life of Jesus, you can find him engaging with the Father by walking in each of the nine pathways that we will discuss in this study. Choose one of the Gospels (Matthew, Mark, Luke, or John) and review it in the coming week while looking for various ways Jesus drew near to his Father. Keep a record of examples in the space provided below:

Gospel I am reading: _____

Pathways:	Example (and passage):
Naturalist	
Sensate	
Traditionalist	

Pathways:	Example (and passage):
Ascetic	
Activist	
Caregiver	
Enthusiast	
Contemplative	
Intellectual	

JOURNAL

Write down your thoughts and reflections on the following topics:

- How have I seen Christians I respect draw near to God in ways that fit them naturally? Which of the pathways do they seem to walk? How does this bind their heart to the heart of God?

- What encounters, experiences, and events have most connected my heart with God's heart? How can I walk this pathway more often?

- Have there been times when I've felt pressured to spend time with God that simply have not worked for me? What are those ways? How can I be freed from feeling the need to walk that particular pathway?

FOR NEXT WEEK

In preparation for next week, read chapters 3, 4, and 5 of *Sacred Pathways* by Gary Thomas.

THE PATHWAYS OF WONDER

Naturalist, Sensate, and Traditionalist

There are followers of Jesus who draw near to God and grow to love him more when they are in awe and amazed by who God is, what he does, and all God has made.

Naturalists *say, "Let me be outdoors."*
Sensates *declare, "Let me experience."*
Traditionalists *cry out, "Let me remember."*

INTRODUCTION

The sun rises and sets every day. Some mornings a sunrise is ordinary. At other times it is breathtaking. Every evening the sun sets. The colors can be staggering and beautiful.

Some people go through life with their eyes focused on the road ahead, their nose to the proverbial grindstone, and their head turned downward. This is not a criticism . . . it is just the way some people are wired. Christians who live with their eyes turned upward, their senses alert to daily surprises, and who appreciate the beauty of a sunrise and sunset will connect with God powerfully through experiences of *wonder*. The crashing of waves on the shore, the beauty of a painting or sculpture, the rhythm of partaking in the elements of communion . . . these things open their eyes to God's presence, power, and goodness.

Walking the pathways of wonder can help a person notice that God is near . . . all the time. A hummingbird in flight declares the intricate design of the Creator of all things. The sweet taste of fruit on a hot summer day or the crunch of a fresh-picked apple on a beautiful fall day can cause one to whisper, "God, you are so good." The booming sound of a church organ playing the prelude to a familiar and much-loved hymn can unleash memories of past worship experiences and cause a heart to soar into the presence of God almighty.

Those who walk the pathways of wonder are truly blessed. They honor God and are swept into his presence again and again by his awesome beauty, his creative nature, and his love for rhythm. Our God is the One who delights to make the sun rise and set every day. And the next day, he joyfully cries out, "Let's do it again!"

TALK ABOUT IT

If you or any of your group members are just meeting for the first time, take a few minutes to introduce yourselves and share any insights you have from last week's personal study. Then, to kick things off, discuss one of the following questions:

- When was a time you were struck by the wonder of God when you saw, heard, or experienced something that displayed his glory?

— *or* —

- How might slowing down during the day and noticing the awe and wonder of God at work in the world deepen your faith in him?

When we see God accurately, we should stand in wonder.

TEACHING NOTES

As you watch the video for this session, use the following outline to record any thoughts or concepts that stand out to you.

Wonder is everywhere if we pay attention (a tour of NASA)

The three pathways of wonder

*The pathway of the **naturalist***

    Biblical example . . .

    People who walk this pathway . . .

    How naturalists connect with God . . .

*The pathway of the **sensate***

    Biblical example . . .

People who walk this pathway . . .

How sensates connect with God . . .

The pathway of the traditionalist

Biblical example . . .

People who walk this pathway . . .

How traditionalists connect with God . . .

The pathways of wonder help us live in awe of a wonderful God

GROUP DISCUSSION

Take a few minutes with your group members to discuss what you just watched and explore these concepts in Scripture.

1. Think about a time you heard, felt, smelled, saw, or tasted something that touched you deep in your soul. How did this amazing experience draw you closer to God?

2. Describe an experience you had in a church service or faith-based gathering when you did something you had done many times before, but God really showed up and touched your heart. How did God reveal himself in that experience?

When we look at art, we learn something about the artist. When we look at creation, we discover new things about the Creator.

3. **Read Psalm 19:1–4.** Naturalists encounter God and draw close to him through engaging with his creation. How does God speak through what he has made? How can this pathway connect you to the heart of God?

4. **Read Psalm 23.** This psalm paints an inviting and inspiring picture using images from creation. If you experienced God in ways reflected in this psalm, how might this draw you closer to your Creator? What are some lessons you can learn from being in God's creation that would be hard to learn in a formal church service or Bible class?

5. Sensates meet God through full engagement of their senses. Think about a time that a painting, sculpture, musical composition, worship song, or a great meal connected you with God in a deep way. How have you encountered God through one of your senses?

6. **Read Ezekiel 1:4–14** and **26–28** and take note of what Ezekiel *feels* and *sees*. **Read Ezekiel 1:24** and **3:12–13** and notice the engagement of his *ears* and sense of *hearing*. **Read Ezekiel 3:1–3** and take note of how he describes the *taste* of the scroll. How did God engage Ezekiel's senses? What example does this give you as you encounter God?

7. Music is a central theme all through the Bible. The longest book in the Bible (Psalms) is actually a collection of songs. How does music and sound touch your heart and help you encounter God's love, power, and truth? What is a particular song that truly stirs your soul and launches you into the presence of God?

*Ritual and symbols draw some people
to Jesus . . . celebrate this!*

8. Smells can trigger memories or sweep you away to a different place in your mind. Tell about a time you smelled something that triggered deep memories and feelings. When was a time this happened in a way that drew you into the presence of God?

9. Rituals, rhythms, symbols, and familiar liturgies draw many people right into the throne room of God. How has a ritual you have taken part in many times or a symbol you have seen often helped you turn your heart toward God?"

10. Symbols, sacred places, and holy routines can act as triggers to bring God's presence and goodness to mind. Talk about each of these possible rhythms and how each might deepen your faith. Then, take time as a group and add a few more ideas to this list:

- Every time you drive by a church building in your community, say a prayer for the congregation to experience God's grace and love in a fresh new way.

- Each time someone engages you in a political conversation, invite those you are with to join you in a simple prayer taught by Jesus: "*Your kingdom come, your will be done, on earth as it is in heaven*" (Matthew 6:10).

- Each time you leave a time of worship, quietly ask the Holy Spirit to help you take one thing you learned and carry it into the coming week.

- When you see a cross (on a person's neck, on top of a church, or in an unexpected place), make a proclamation in your heart or out loud: "I will take up the cross of Jesus and follow him this day and every day!"

"You will find something more in woods than in books. Trees and stones will teach you that which you can never learn from masters."
SAINT BERNARD OF CLAIRVAUX

CLOSING PRAYER

Spend time as your group comes to a close to pray in some of the following directions:

- Thank God for the beauty of his creation and ask him to help you notice his presence, beauty, and glory in what he has made. Pray that the wonder of God's handiwork would move you to worship.

- Express gratitude to God for the variety and wonder of your senses. Pray for a deeper awareness of how God can draw near to you through sights, smells, sounds, touch, and all that is around you.

- Ask the Holy Spirit to draw you into the sacred rhythms of worship and life. Ask him to show the face of Jesus in these routines.

For the true Christian naturalist, creation is nothing less than a sanctuary—a holy place that invites you to prayer.

BETWEEN-SESSIONS PERSONAL STUDY

Reflect on the content you've covered this week in *Sacred Pathways* by engaging in any or all of the following between-sessions activities. The time you invest will be well spent, so let God use it to draw you closer to him. At your next meeting, share with your group any key points or insights that stood out to you as you spent this time with the Lord.

WALK THE PATHWAY OF A NATURALIST . . . LITERALLY!

Take a walk in creation. If you have the courage to do so, turn off your phone or even leave it in your car or house. Slow down, notice, and thank God for his infinite creativity. You might want to ask God questions while you walk and look closer at some things in creation you often rush past. Write down some observations of how you saw God and experienced his presence.

Any place that has some trees or a stream or, at minimum, open skies, can be God's cathedral.

SOAK IT IN AND SOAK IN IT

If you have a bathtub (or a hot tub), find a time you won't be interrupted and just have a nice soak. Add in some great music that touches your soul and connects you to God. If you want to add one more sense into the mix, go with scented candles, bubble bath, or a bath bomb. You might find yourself feeling closer to God than you have in a long time! Once again, write down some observations of how you saw God and experienced his presence as you did this.

CARRY IT WITH YOU

Carry a reminder for a week (be sure you can feel it). This could be a rock that reminds you of David's victory over Goliath, a nail that reminds you of Jesus' sacrifice on the cross, a small cross that turns your mind to the call to follow Jesus no matter what the cost, or some other pocket-sized reminder that you can hold, touch, use as a memento of a biblical truth or God's presence with you. Write down any thoughts below that run through your mind, and the ways you feel God's presence, as you think about this object. As a bonus, tell someone else how you encountered God through this simple exercise and practice.

KEEP A CALENDAR

Place a calendar somewhere in your home and add the key dates of the church year. If you are not familiar with these, do a quick online search on Christian festivals and holy days. If there are any you don't recognize, do a search on that particular day and learn what it is about. (You can also add these to your computer or phone calendar.) Write your notes on what you find below.

Through the coming year, seek to learn about and observe the wonder and meaning of these days—Advent, Ascension Day, Christmas, Easter, Epiphany, Good Friday, Lent, Ash Wednesday, and more. It might even be fun to do this with your small group and share what you are learning. If anyone asks you about the extra holidays on your calendar, describe what they mean to you and how they connect you to your Savior.

JOURNAL

Write down your thoughts and reflections on the following topics:

- How do I encounter God and feel closer to him in creation? What specific places really cry out to me with God's presence and power?

- Where do I feel numb and cut off from God? How can I open my senses up to God's voice, touch, and presence?

- What are traditions that don't really work for me? What are the ones that seem to open my eyes and heart to experience the wonder and awe of God?

FOR NEXT WEEK

In preparation for next week, read chapters 6, 10, and 11 of *Sacred Pathways* by Gary Thomas.

THE PATHWAYS OF CONTEMPLATION

Intellectual, Ascetic, and Contemplative

There are lovers of Jesus who yearn for quiet. Their soul connects to God in spaces where they can reflect, find solitude, and plumb the depths of their emotional world.

Intellectuals *say, "Let me think."*
Ascetics *request, "Let me be alone."*
Contemplatives *ask, "Let me feel."*

INTRODUCTION

We live in a busy, driven, frenetic world with jam-packed schedules and "to do" lists as long as the day. Being overextended can be worn as a badge of honor. Many people find such an existence of constant action and activity to be appealing. In fact, many churches today cater to such individuals. Worship experiences are filled with great songs, visuals, and messages. Bible studies, youth events, and children's programs provide amazing content. Everything is kept structured and orderly to make sure to "maximize" the congregation's time.

Unfortunately, these scheduled programs can fail to make space for silence, reflection, or response. They can leave out those people who need space to process what they are seeing, hearing, and learning. Some Jesus followers just need *time* to ponder the truths that they encounter in the Scriptures or a song. They need the solitude of time alone to meet with God. In this space, the noise melts away and they experience God's presence in their hearts.

Those who walk the pathways of contemplation find their minds are quickened by the presence of the Holy Spirit as Scripture comes alive, theology unfolds, truth inspires, and meaning moves their heart. As they meet with God in such times of solitude and silence, they sense God's presence and hear his whispers of love, grace, hope, and truth. The God who made us and delights to be with us draws near to those who long for a touch from his hand—and the church is enriched through these disciples who dare to think deeply, pull away from the crowd, and fully engage their hearts.

TALK ABOUT IT

Begin your group time by inviting anyone to share his or her insights from last week's personal study. Next, to kick things off, discuss one of the following questions:

- When was a time you encountered God and experienced his presence in quiet and contemplation?

— or —

- How might making space for reflection, solitude, or feelings connect you more intimately with God?

All people who walk the pathways of contemplation like quiet, but they like it for different reasons.

TEACHING NOTES

As you watch the video for this session, use the following outline to record any thoughts or concepts that stand out to you.

Learning from children . . . we are all wired differently!

The three pathways of contemplation

*The pathway of the **intellectual***

    Biblical example . . .

    People who walk this pathway . . .

    How intellectuals connect with God . . .

*The pathway of the **ascetic***

    Biblical example . . .

People who walk this pathway . . .

How ascetics connect with God . . .

**Some Christians see God as their dearest love
and One to spend time with more than One to
be served, understood, or even celebrated.**

---

*The pathway of the **contemplative***

Biblical example . . .

People who walk this pathway . . .

How contemplatives connect with God . . .

The deep wells of the Church

---

*Some Christians see God as their dearest love
and One to spend time with more than One to
be served, understood, or even celebrated.*

GROUP DISCUSSION

Take a few minutes with your group members to discuss what you just watched and explore these concepts in Scripture.

1. When was a time you learned a new truth about God and that deeper level of understanding made you feel closer and more in love with your Savior?

2. **Read Romans 12:1–2.** How can renewing your mind, learning new things, and gaining new understanding about your faith take you to new places in your relationship with God? How can renewing your mind connect you closer to the heart of your God?

Don't be misled by the title "intellectual." It simply describes those believers whose hearts are most warmed toward God when they understand new concepts and gain new insights and increased comprehension.

---

3. What are some important biblical truths you need to be reminded of frequently? How do reminders of these truths draw you closer to God and help you to follow him?

4. Some Christians feel that pulling away from others and seeking solitude is insensitive and even a bit selfish. But how can making time to step away from the busyness of the world to meet with Christ actually make you more sensitive and caring toward others?

5. **Read Exodus 24:1–4 and 15–18.** How did Moses enter a time of solitude? What did God do through this time? How has the world benefited from Moses' willingness to seek the face of God in isolation and quiet?

6. **Read Mark 6:30–32.** What did Jesus instruct the disciples to do in this passage? What does this tell you about the importance of having times of solitude and rest?

*Jesus was emphatic that the spiritual
life is based on love, not laws.*

7. **Read Psalm 63.** How do you see David express his love, passion, and intimacy to God? When was a time you felt such a deep emotional connection with God?

8. Think about a Christian you know and respect who loves God with a level of personal passion and intimacy that inspires you. How does that person connect with God? What have you learned from his or her example and spiritual journey?

9. What are some of the unique and valuable things a contemplative Christian can bring to the family of God?

10. What is one step you can take to explore and experience the contemplative pathways to see if these three ways of connecting with God resonate for you?

There is one thing that each of us as Christians can do that nobody else can—give our personal love and affection to God.

CLOSING PRAYER

Spend time as your group comes to a close to pray in some of the following directions:

- Thank God for those believers who meet God in the quiet of their mind. Pray that they will explore even deeper places of intimacy through exercising their intellect and then share what they learn with people around them.

- Lift up prayers celebrating your brothers and sisters whose hearts connect with God through rich intimacy and expressions of intense love. Pray that they will hear God's words of affection and affirmation.

- Pray for those who meet God in times when they are in the quiet of solitude. Ask that they would be able to find those places for deep connection to God. Thank God for how they model the beauty of being intimate with Jesus and stir those around them to continue to grow in their own intimacy with him.

There is love and devotion that only you can give God!

BETWEEN-SESSIONS PERSONAL STUDY

Reflect on the content you've covered this week in *Sacred Pathways* by engaging in any or all of the following between-sessions activities. The time you invest will be well spent, so let God use it to draw you closer to him. At your next meeting, share with your group any key points or insights that stood out to you as you spent this time with the Lord.

READ AND REFLECT

Take time in the coming week to engage your mind by reading one of the following chapters of the Bible or portions of one of the books recommended below:

- Chapters 1, 2, or 3 from the book of Ecclesiastes
- Chapters 1, 2, 3, 4, 8, or 10 from the book of Proverbs
- Chapters 1, 2, 6, 9, 11, 53, or 58, from the book of Isaiah
- Chapters 1, 2, 3, 7, 9, or 10 from the book of Acts
- Bruce Shelly, *Church History in Plain Language* (Thomas Nelson, 2013)
- Clyde Manschreck, *A History of Christianity* (Prentice-Hall, 1965)
- Gordon Fee and Douglas Stuart, *How to Read the Bible for All Its Worth* (Zondervan, 2014)
- J.I. Packer, *Concise Theology* (Tyndale House, 2001)

What are a few new things you learned about God after doing this reading?

How do these truths inspire your heart, grow your love for God, or make you want to walk more intimately with your Creator?

Make time in the next week to share one of these new insights with someone in your life who also loves to think deeply about things of faith.

*Intellectuals remind us of the high
calling of loving God with our mind.*

EXPERIMENT WITH CONTEMPLATION

Try one of these exercises to help you focus your attention on God and reflect more deeply on his presence with you:

- Stay up for a couple of hours one night during this up-coming week for the express purpose of being silent and listening for God to speak to you. Write down notes about whispers you hear, nudges you feel, and impressions you sense God is giving you.

- Take a silent retreat (ranging from two hours to a day). In this time, do not speak or communicate (even by a computer or phone). Read Scripture, pray, be quiet, meditate on biblical passages, and invite God to speak to you.

- Fast from one meal or all meals for twenty-four hours. Each time you feel hunger pains or hear your stomach growl, reflect on how God satisfies your deepest needs and quenches your greatest thirst.

- Do a media fast, where you stay off social media and all entertainment media (including games) for one to three days. Keep notes of how this discipline helps you focus on God and feel his presence with greater clarity.

- Experiment with simplicity. Find a place you can meet with God each day for a week. Make this place as simple and spartan as you can. Remove all clutter and distractions (including technology), and only place things around you in this space that will turn your thoughts and heart to Jesus.

Which of these exercises did you choose? Why did you select that particular one to do during this week?

What insights and lessons did you learn by going through this particular spiritual exercise?

Take time at your next small group gathering to share one of your insights from this exercise.

The almost unbelievable joy is that you can enjoy
a relationship with God that he will have with
no one else. And God eagerly and passionately
yearns for that relationship to begin.

SIMPLE AND RICH REPETITION

For centuries, there have been faithful followers of Jesus who have learned to draw near to him through simple repetitions of a prayer or a declaration of faith. Today, follow their example by lifting a simple prayer or faith-declaration each time you have a little space in your day. Try one of the examples below, or write your own prayer or declaration of faith.

PRAYER OPTIONS

- Lord Jesus Christ, Son of God, Have mercy on me, a sinner.
- God of kindness, lavish me with your grace.
- Spirit of truth, open my ears, mind, and heart to receive and embrace your truth.

Your prayer . . .

PRAISE AND THANKSGIVING OPTIONS

- Spirit of the Living God, thank you for comforting me in my times of need.
- Sovereign God, I praise you for protecting me and guiding me every day.

- Lord Jesus, merciful and loving friend, I praise you for being near me always.

Your praise . . .

DECLARATION

- My God . . . Father, Son, and Holy Spirit, you alone are my Lord and Hope.
- Lord Jesus, you are my God, my friend, my greatest delight.
- God Almighty, you are my fortress, my mighty tower, and my solid rock.

Your declaration of truth . . .

A SONG, POEM, OR LOVE LETTER

You may love this next exercise, or you may just chuckle and say, "This one is not for me." Either way is fine. In the space below, write a song, a poem, or a letter directly to the God who loves you. Express your heart and feelings to God as the lover of your soul.

If you are comfortable doing so, share this with a Christian you trust and respect. You might even want to share this with your group members the next time you meet.

JOURNAL

Write down your thoughts and reflections on the following topics:

- As you get to know more about the various pathways to intimacy with God, write a prayer asking God to help you embrace and celebrate the ways that other Christians connect most meaningfully with God.

- If you have found the pathways of contemplation do not connect for you, write down a few reasons why you feel these pathways can be of value to specific people you love who seem to connect to God through these pathways. You might even want to write a prayer for God to draw these people closer as they walk pathways that fit them.

- Make a list of people you believe would benefit by knowing more about the three pathways of contemplation. Write down three or four lessons you could share with them about drawing near to God through walking these pathways.

FOR NEXT WEEK

In preparation for next week, read chapters 7, 8, and 9 of *Sacred Pathways* by Gary Thomas.

THE PATHWAYS OF ACTION

Caregiver, Activist, and Enthusiast

The Spirit of God has super-charged some Christians with energy and desire to do things for Jesus. These passionate believers feel the pleasure of God and are most engaged in their faith when they are doing something that honors God.

*The **Caregiver** says, "Let me care."*
*The **Activist** says, "Let me conquer."*
*The **Enthusiast** says, "Let me celebrate."*

INTRODUCTION

It happens every ninety-minutes . . . give or take ten minutes. It is explosive and powerful. Since its discovery in 1870, this natural phenomenon has amazed and delighted crowds with a predictability that is simply staggering. People today gather around it, watching and waiting. Hearts race. Then, all of a sudden, the water bursts from the ground and gushes heavenward, rising 106 feet to 185 feet in the air. This geothermal eruption has happened more than a million times since the first explorers saw it and appropriately named it *Old Faithful.*

Predictable and *powerful.* These words describe the geyser— and they describe Christians who walk the pathways of action. These followers of Christ erupt into action that unleashes the compassion of Jesus to a broken and hurting world. They *feel* deeply, and then they *do* something about it. Some see injustice and inequity, and something bubbles up inside them. They can't hold it back. A Holy Spirit-prompted eruption of planning, action, words, and service brings heaven to earth, and the grace of Jesus is felt as things change and the kingdom of God breaks into real life situations. Joy and excitement grow until they simply can't be held back. Worship explodes, heaven delights, and the world watches on as Jesus is lifted up.

If you have ever been to Old Faithful, you could probably close your eyes right now and picture it. It is deeply memorable. In the same way, when you walk the pathways of action, your life will be the source of regular and predictable eruptions of compassion, action, and celebration. The people around you will get used to it. They will expect it. And the world will look on, with "oohhs and ahhhs," and be amazed at the way God's divine activity is unleashed through a person who walks one of these powerful pathways.

The mystery of faith calls us to love and serve
a God whom we can't always understand.

TALK ABOUT IT

Begin your group time by inviting anyone to share his or her insights from last week's personal study. Next, to kick things off, discuss one of the following questions:

- If you have ever seen Old Faithful, how would you describe the awe and the wonder of this God-made phenomenon?

  — or —

- If you have been around a person who is moved to God-honoring action on a regular basis, how have you seen God glorified through his or her life?

All Christians are called to care for the poor and hurting,
but caregivers do it out of a hunger to meet God.

TEACHING NOTES

As you watch the video for this session, use the following outline to record any thoughts or concepts that stand out to you.

Eruptions, explosions, and things that move us into action

The three pathways of action

*The pathway of the **caregiver***

Biblical example . . .

People who walk this pathway . . .

How caregivers connect with God . . .

*The pathway of the **activist***

    Biblical example . . .

    People who walk this pathway . . .

    How activists connect with God . . .

*The pathway of the **enthusiast***

    Biblical example . . .

    People who walk this pathway . . .

How enthusiasts connect with God . . .

The pathways of action point us beyond ourselves

---

*Enthusiasts believe in the mystery
of God—and they love to celebrate it!*

GROUP DISCUSSION

Take a few minutes with your group members to discuss what you
just watched and explore these concepts in Scripture.

1. Some people encounter Jesus when they are caring for
   those who are broken, hurting, and in need. Why do you
   think caregivers encounter Jesus in such a deep way when
   they are extending compassion to those who are often for-
   gotten and marginalized?

2. **Read James 1:27.** Caregivers would lift up a hearty "Amen!" to these words from James. Why is this kind of care a beautiful picture of true religion that honors God?

In a tangible way, the caregiver is a witness to God's existence by demonstrating his love through the giving of care.

---

3. Caregiving can take many shapes and forms. It can be caring for a family member in need, repairing cars for those struggling financially, preparing and serving meals to the hungry, offering to take care of the church grounds as a volunteer . . . the list goes on. When was a time that you had the privilege of serving and helping to meet a need? How did you encounter God through that act of service?

4. **Read Exodus 2:11–12, 16–19; 10:24–26; 20:18–21.** How do you see Moses as an example of a person who took action for God each time he saw a need that could be met or injustice that could be corrected?

> *Activists don't pick a fight for the sake of fighting,*
> *but they are not afraid of conflict if it leads to*
> *accomplishing the will of God in our world.*

5. Many of the greatest activists in the history of the church were people who believed in the power of prayer and who called others to prayer while they moved them to action. Why do you think prayer and action are so often bound up in the life of the same person? What are ways you can add more prayer to the actions you take for Christ?

6. One of the ways a Christian can be an activist is through passionate evangelism. How is sharing your faith with those who are far from God a needed and important behavior of activism? Who is one person in your circle of influence who needs to know the love and grace of Jesus? How can your group members pray for that person?

7. **Read Acts 26:19–29.** When you think of the life of the apostle Paul, what are some signs and indicators that he was a serious activist? What were some of the world-changing results of Paul's activism?

8. Jesus is a powerful example of all nine of the sacred pathways. How do you see the pathway of an activist in the life of Jesus? How have the actions of Jesus changed the world and your personal life?

---

*We can't expect to faithfully serve God
and be liked by his enemies.*

---

9. In Old Testament times, there were many feasts the people of God celebrated. Why is celebration, rejoicing, and delighting in God's goodness an important part of the Christian faith? When was a time you took part in a meaningful Christian celebration? How did that experience bring you closer to God?

10. Christians who walk the pathways of action meet God in activity, movement, and engagement. Why are these people so needed in the church and world today? How does their action show others the presence of God?

CLOSING PRAYER

Spend time as your group comes to a close to pray in some of the following directions:

- Thank God for the believers who have extended care and compassion in your church, your community, and around the world. Be sure to pray for specific people and acts of care.

- Pray for believers you know who are taking action to right wrongs and overcome injustice. Ask for the power of the Holy Spirit to fill them and make them effective in each action they take for Jesus.

- Invite the Holy Spirit to fill the enthusiasts who are part of your church to be an example of deep praise and joyful celebration. Pray that they will inspire others, including yourself, to go to deeper places of praise and worship.

The act of celebration reminds us that
we have much to be thankful for.

BETWEEN-SESSIONS PERSONAL STUDY

Reflect on the content you've covered this week in *Sacred Pathways* by engaging in any or all of the following between-sessions activities. The time you invest will be well spent, so let God use it to draw you closer to him. At your next meeting, share with your group any key points or insights that stood out to you as you spent this time with the Lord.

HOW CAN I HELP?

Every local church has lonely people who would love a visit, struggling people who need help in some way, and projects that serve the whole church. Take time to find out some of the needs in your church that involve caring. (You will discover that some of these needs are within your church and others are in your local community.) Read your church bulletin, review the church website, or call your church and ask if there are ways that you can help and extend care. Record these in the space below. You will be surprised at the opportunities that are just waiting to be met!

Once you have your list, pick one that you can do this week. As you care and serve, take note of how you feel God's presence and pleasure. How does this act draw your heart closer to Jesus, the most caring being in the universe? Write down a few of your observations here.

It is one thing to say we believe: it's another to show compassion to others, to inconvenience ourselves because we believe.

COMMUNITY PROJECT

Find a community-based project that involves care for the hurting or action that will right a wrong. Then, as a small group, engage in this project or ministry at least twice during the coming six to eight weeks. As you do this, remember that while some followers of Jesus walk this pathway naturally, *all* Christians are called to extend compassion and make a difference in the world. After you have engaged in this Jesus-honoring action, spend a little time debriefing as a group and discuss the following questions. Write down some of the lessons you learn.

How did this experience make you feel closer to God as you partnered with your group members in this action?

Did this action come naturally to you or did you have to work on staying engaged and excited about it (be honest—we are all wired differently)?

How did you sense the presence of Jesus in you, around you, or working in the lives of others as you took part in this action?

PLAN A FEAST

Take an evening as a small group and have a big meal together. (You might even want to invite a few other people to join you.) During the meal, read Bible passages you love, and ask others to read a favorite passage and share what it means to them. Have the members play a worship song and share why it leads them into the presence of God. Spend time lifting up prayers of praise and thanksgiving—and lift up prayers for God to move Christians into the world with actions that honor Jesus. Do these things around the table while you have a slow and leisurely meal together.

JOURNAL

Write down your thoughts and reflections on the following topics:

- How was Jesus an activist? What were some ways Jesus battled wrong and stood against systems that hurt the people he loved?

- How was Jesus a caregiver? What are ways you see Jesus extending care, compassion, and tender love to those who were hurting and in need?

- What are some of the things that cause you to be enthusiastic about your faith and passionate in how you worship Jesus?

FOR NEXT WEEK

In preparation for next week, your final session in this study, read chapter 12 of *Sacred Pathways* by Gary Thomas.

TENDING THE GARDEN OF THE SOUL

How the Pathways Apply to Your Life

A garden with only one kind of flower is boring. When you see the wide array of colors and shapes that God has made in flowers, and when you put these together in a garden, it is a beautiful testimony to the creativity of our Maker. The same is true with how God made people and the spiritual pathways we walk. As each unique Christian walks his or her God-designed pathway, the beauty of God's plan unfolds for heaven and earth to see.

INTRODUCTION

As you think about the nine pathways, there are three words that can guide your journey forward: *all, some, one*. If you follow these three words, God will unleash fresh new experiences of his presence, peace, and power in your life, the church, and the world.

All. Commit yourself to celebrate all of the pathways. God made them, and Jesus modeled them, so you can trust that each pathway honors God and draws people nearer to him. You will certainly find that some of the pathways do not connect well for you. They might even seem odd or feel less spiritual. But choose to humbly embrace *all* of the pathways and rejoice in the diverse ways your brothers and sisters walk with Jesus. You can affirm another believers' journey—even when it is not how you prefer to connect with God.

Some. Make a decision to more deeply explore the pathways that seem to fit with how God has uniquely wired you. As you've studied the pathways, there were likely three of four that felt familiar and even exciting to you. As you listened, it became clear that you have already walked a few of the pathways before you had a name for them. You might have even thought, "I might want to explore that pathway a bit more." This is wonderful! Commit to experiment, try some of the exercises at the end of each session, and dig deeper into some new pathways.

One. Develop one of the pathways that you know for certain fits you. If you took the assessment at the beginning of this study, you already know at least one pathway that especially draws you close to Jesus. Your soul will soar when you walk this pathway. Don't fight it. Keep developing it. As you explore other ways to go deeper in your relationship with the Savior, you will always this have one that you know connects you to God naturally.

So . . . celebrate *all* nine of the sacred pathways as a gift from your creative God. Seek to go deeper in *some* of the pathways that fit the way God has made you. Lean into *one* of the pathways that really draws you to the heart of God, and keep building on that pathway to make it as strong as it can be. Most of all, be sure to understand all of the pathways so that you can encourage all followers of Jesus to grow deeper in their faith and more in love with Christ.

Discerning our strong tendencies and predominant spiritual temperament gives us the information we need to construct a comprehensive plan for spiritual growth.

TALK ABOUT IT

Begin your group time by inviting anyone to share his or her insights from last week's personal study. Next, to kick things off, discuss one of the following questions:

- What have you learned in this study that has helped you understand and affirm pathways that you have not really thought about before?

— or —

- What are some pathways that you have not walked through much, but feel you should now explore as you grow in your relationship with Jesus?

TEACHING NOTES

As you watch the video for this session, use the following outline to record any thoughts or concepts that stand out to you.

The story of the family well . . . keep the water flowing

A review of the sacred pathways:

    *Pathways of **wonder***

        The naturalist says, let me . . .

        The sensate says, let me . . .

The traditionalist says, let me . . .

Pathways of **contemplation**

The intellectual says, let me . . .

The ascetic says, let me . . .

The contemplative says, let me . . .

Pathways of **action**

The caregiver says, let me . . .

The activist says, let me . . .

The enthusiast says, let me . . .

Accept your pathway(s)

Accept the pathway(s) of others

Tend your garden

Looking more and more like Jesus as you walk closely with him

Write your own prescription for how you best meet with God

Help others on how to connect best with God

---

*The invitation is to relate with
God and reflect his glory.*

GROUP DISCUSSION

Take a few minutes with your group members to discuss what you just watched and explore these concepts in Scripture.

1. Think about what you have learned about the nine unique pathways during this study. How has this helped you understand how followers of Jesus can meet with him in a variety of ways that fit how God has uniquely made each of us?

2. How has this study helped you affirm and deepen the way you meet with the Savior?

3. During the teaching, you heard the story about a pastor of a large church who wanted to have a different pathway. He wanted to be an ascetic, but he had to embrace the reality that he was an activist. If you felt this way (wishing you had a different pathway) at some point during this group study, share your story. Why is it so important to honestly identify the pathways that fit you and seek to walk in them?

Don't fall into pathway envy, and don't deny the world who God made you to be!

4. Some people connect with a pathway for a period of time, but then discover another pathway that resonates with them and draws them close to God in another season. If you look back and discover this has been the case in your spiritual life, how have the different pathways served you well at different times?

5. Although we have many ways to draw near to God, we all need to open the Bible and learn from God's revelation and truth. Take some time as a group to look at how engaging Scripture can be a natural part of each of the pathways:

- Naturalist

- Sensate

- Traditionalist

- Intellectual

- Ascetic

- Contemplative

- Caregiver

- Activist

- Enthusiast

How can each of these pathways provide a valuable means to feed on Scripture?

6. Something beautiful happens when Christians who walk different pathways work together, learn together, and cheer each other on. How could people with the following pairings work together to go places spiritually that they might not go on their own?

- An activist and a caregiver

- An enthusiast and a traditionalist

- A naturalist and a contemplative

- Any other pairing . . .

7. Imagine your small group was given the task of planning worship services for your church. As a group, you decide to integrate at least one worship element that would touch the people who walk each of the nine sacred pathways. What elements would you recommend to be sure there was a touchpoint for every person?

8. Think about what it would be like to serve at a banquet when you were super hungry. Now think about how different you would feel if you had just finished eating and felt satisfied. How is this a picture of the importance of being filled

spiritually? What are one or two steps you can take to be sure you are letting God fill you up?

9. Jesus had a place he went to meet with the Father—the Garden of Gethsemane held a special place in the life of our Savior. Where do you meet with God (this can be a literal or figurative place)? What do you do when you are there? How does God charge your batteries and strengthen your soul when you meet with him in this place?

Draw near to God and he will draw near to you.
JAMES 4:8

---

10. What is your next step to grow deeper in one of the sacred pathways? How can your group members pray for you and cheer you on as you seek to connect more closely with God through walking this pathway?

TAKE THE ASSESSMENT

Close out your time in this study by retaking the personal assessment found in the back of this guide. Go through the assessment, tally your score, and compare against the assessment you took at the beginning of the study. Discuss any differences you find in your particular pathways with your group members and why those results might have changed for you.

CLOSING PRAYER

Spend time as your group comes to a close to pray in some of the following directions:

- Thank God for his creative beauty in the way he has made the other members of your group. Pray for them to continue developing their unique pathway to intimacy with Jesus.

- Ask God to help you discover one or two fresh new ways to grow spiritually as you explore new pathways that could fit how God has made you.

- Ask the Holy Spirit to help you understand all of the pathways so you can affirm other believers who connect with God in ways different than you.

- Pray for the leaders of your church as they design worship services, learning opportunities, children's programs, the youth ministry, and more. Ask God to lead them in ways that will develop meaningful opportunities for growth that embrace all nine of the sacred pathways.

BETWEEN-SESSIONS PERSONAL STUDY

Reflect on the content you've covered this week in *Sacred Pathways* by engaging in any or all of the following between-sessions activities. The time you invest will be well spent, so let God use it to draw you closer to him. In the coming weeks, be sure to share with your group members any key points or insights that stood out to you as you spent this time with the Lord.

OBSERVE AND SHARE WHAT YOU HAVE LEARNED

Seek to be a student of other followers of Christ. Pay attention to how they live, pursue Jesus, and connect with God. If you notice those who seem to be enthusiasts, share what you have learned about their pathway. It will be encouraging for them and give language to how they grow in their intimacy with God. If they are caregivers, bless it, celebrate it, and share what you have learned about that pathway. When you observe activists, tell them that you love how God uses them, and then ask about how they meet God in their action. Do the same for the other pathways. Encourage each person to go deeper, and maybe challenge them to jump into a small group and go through this study.

PARTNER UP!

If you notice a friend has a pathway that could supplement and support your pathway, talk about how you could learn from each other, encourage each other, and even serve the church or world in some way. God loves to see his children walk together in harmony and bear fruit for his glory. So let the sacred pathways become a place where you walk with other believers toward Jesus and into the world for his glory. Too often we look at our spiritual growth as something that happens in isolation. Discover the joy of growing in community.

Every true spiritual path has Jesus Christ at its center, but in Christ there are many ways for us to express our faith.

ENCOURAGE YOUR CHURCH LEADERS

If you feel it would be helpful, share what you have learned in *Sacred Pathways* with one of your church leaders and how it has impacted your spiritual growth. Be humble in how you share, but encourage the person to discover the importance of recognizing there are many people in every ministry of the church who learn in ways that might not fit the "normal" programmatic planning and process. Then pray that this leader will discover the joy and beauty of planning ministry that touches people who walk each of the pathways.

JOURNAL

Write down your thoughts and reflections on the following topics:

- When did I notice a fellow believer walking one of the sacred pathways? How did I encourage or affirm that person?

- What is my primary pathway? How can I walk it with increasing passion as I seek to grow in my relationship with Jesus?

- What are pathways that might fit me? How can I explore and experiment with finding new ways to grow closer to God as I walk one of these pathways?

SACRED PATHWAYS
ASSESSMENT

The following exercise will help you determine which of the nine sacred pathways is dominant in your life. Read each of the 45 statements below and circle or place an "X" over the number to the right that reflects the degree to which you agree or disagree with that statement. Your choices are 1 to 5, with 1 being the lowest level of agreement and 5 being the highest:

5   I completely agree with this statement
4   I mostly agree with this statement
3   I go either way as to whether I agree or disagree
2   I mostly disagree with this statement
1   I completely disagree with this statement

After recording your responses, follow the instructions for scoring at the end of the assessment.

I feel closest to God when . . .

Disagree   Agree

1. I'm surrounded by what he has made and can experience it—the mountains, the forests, the ocean.

   1 2 3 4 5

2. I'm in a church that allows my senses to come alive—when I can see, smell, hear, and almost taste his majesty.

   1 2 3 4 5

3. I'm participating in a form of worship that has memories dating back to my childhood. Traditions move me more than anything else.

   1 2 3 4 5

4. I'm alone and there is nothing to distract me from focusing on his presence.

   1 2 3 4 5

5. I'm standing up for his justice—writing letters to officials, attending rallies for causes, urging people to vote, becoming informed about current issues.

   1 2 3 4 5

6. I'm sitting by the bed of someone who is lonely or ill, or taking a meal to someone in need, or offering a ride or volunteering for helping activities.

   1 2 3 4 5

7. I'm celebrating God and his love. At such times my heart is sent soaring and I feel like I want to burst, worship God all day long, and shout out his name.

   1 2 3 4 5

8. My emotions are awakened—when God touches my heart, tells me that he loves me, and makes me feel like I'm his closest friend.

   1 2 3 4 5

9. My mind is stimulated and I learn something about God that I didn't understand before. It is important to me that I know exactly what I believe.

   1 2 3 4 5

I am most energized in my faith when . . .

Disagree   Agree

10. I am able to spend my time outdoors rather than just listening to speakers or singing songs in a church building. Nothing makes me feel closer to God than just being outside in nature.

1 2 3 4 5

11. I attend a "high church" service with incense and formal Communion or Eucharist.

1 2 3 4 5

12. I can lay something in my life on the altar, sacrificing it for God.

1 2 3 4 5

13. I am able to focus on more of the "internal" than the "external."

1 2 3 4 5

14. I see other Christians actively engaged in worthwhile causes. I want to drop everything else I'm doing and help the church overcome its apathy.

1 2 3 4 5

15. I see other Christians helping a sick neighbor, or cooking a meal for a family in need, or fixing a car for a struggling family. I grow weary of Christians who spend their time just singing songs while these needs go unmet.

1 2 3 4 5

16. I can take a spiritual risk on behalf of God. Tradition and ritual put me to sleep—I want to see God move in unexpected ways!

1 2 3 4 5

17. I can actively feel God's presence within me.

1 2 3 4 5

18. I receive solid teaching that helps me understand the Christian faith and have proper doctrine. I don't focus on feelings and spiritual experience.

1 2 3 4 5

These terms are most appealing to me . . .	Disagree				Agree
19. God's creation, nature, outdoor scenery	1	2	3	4	5
20. ornate sanctuary, art and music, God's majesty	1	2	3	4	5
21. tradition, rituals, history	1	2	3	4	5
22. silence, solitude, discipline	1	2	3	4	5
23. courageous confrontation, justice, social activism	1	2	3	4	5
24. service, caring for others, compassion	1	2	3	4	5
25. celebration, joy, enthusiasm	1	2	3	4	5
26. lover, intimacy, heart	1	2	3	4	5
27. concepts, doctrine, truth	1	2	3	4	5

I would be most drawn to . . .   Disagree   Agree

28. Escaping to a garden to pray, walking
alone through a meadow, taking a trip to
the mountains to witness beauty in nature.   1   2   3   4   5

29. Going to museums, attending concerts.   1   2   3   4   5

30. A formal liturgy or "prayer book" service,
creating symbols that I can place in my
home or office, developing a Christian
calendar for our family to follow.   1   2   3   4   5

31. Taking an overnight retreat by myself,
spending time alone in a small room,
praying, studying God's Word, fasting.   1   2   3   4   5

32. Confronting a social evil, attending a
meeting of the local school board to
challenge the new curriculum, volunteer-
ing on a political campaign.   1   2   3   4   5

33. Counseling a friend who has lost a job,
preparing meals or fixing the car of a
family in need, spending a week at an
orphanage in Mexico.   1   2   3   4   5

34. Attending a workshop on learning to worship through dance, being part of a worship
session with contemporary music, looking
for God to move in unexpected ways.   1   2   3   4   5

35. Spending thirty minutes each day to sit in
prayer and "hold hands" with God, writing
love letters to him, enjoying his presence.   1   2   3   4   5

36. Participating in a time of uninterrupted
study, reading God's Word or good
Christian books, participating or teaching
in a discussion with a small group.   1   2   3   4   5

When it comes to worship . . .

	Disagree				Agree

37. It is more moving for me to see God's beauty in nature than understand new concepts, attend a formal religious service, or participate in social causes.　　1　2　3　4　5

38. My prayer life is improved when I am surrounded by religious icons or there is classical music playing in the background.　　1　2　3　4　5

39. I feel it is important to develop a personal rule (or ritual) of prayer.　　1　2　3　4　5

40. I would particularly benefit from acts such as a night watch, taking a short vow of silence, or simplifying my life.　　1　2　3　4　5

41. I would rather stand in the rain for an hour to confront an evil than sit in a room for an hour and pray, take a walk through the woods, or spend an hour reading a book.　　1　2　3　4　5

42. I would rather nurse someone to health or help someone repair their house than teach a class, go on a prayer and fasting retreat, or take a lonely walk in the woods.　　1　2　3　4　5

43. It is more moving for me to have worship music available to me.　　1　2　3　4　5

44. I think of God's love, friendship, and adoration more than anything else.　　1　2　3　4　5

45. It is more moving for me to have books available to me.　　1　2　3　4　5

SCORING

Write down the score you recorded for each of the numbered statements. Then add up the columns and record in the "totals" row. The column with the highest number indicates your primary pathway; the next highest number indicates your secondary pathway; and so forth.

	Naturalist	Sensate	Traditionalist
	1 = ____	2 = ____	3 = ____
	10 = ____	11 = ____	12 = ____
	19 = ____	20 = ____	21 = ____
	28 = ____	29 = ____	30 = ____
	37 = ____	38 = ____	39 = ____
TOTAL			

	Ascetic	Activist	Caregiver
	4 = ____	5 = ____	6 = ____
	13 = ____	14 = ____	15 = ____
	22 = ____	23 = ____	24 = ____
	31 = ____	32 = ____	33 = ____
	40 = ____	41 = ____	42 = ____
TOTAL			

	Enthusiast	Contemplative	Intellectual
	7 = ____	8 = ____	9 = ____
	16 = ____	17 = ____	18 = ____
	25 = ____	26 = ____	27 = ____
	34 = ____	35 = ____	36 = ____
	43 = ____	44 = ____	45 = ____
TOTAL			

LEADER'S GUIDE

Thank you for your willingness to lead your group through this study! What you have chosen to do is valuable and will make a great difference in the lives of others. The rewards of being a leader are different from those of participating, and we hope that as you lead you will find your own walk with Jesus deepened by this experience.

Sacred Pathways is a five-session study built around video content and small-group interaction. As the group leader, just think of yourself as the host of a dinner party. Your job is to take care of your guests by managing all the behind-the-scenes details so that when everyone arrives, they can just enjoy time together.

As the group leader, your role is not to answer all the questions or reteach the content—the video, book, and study guide will do most of that work. Your job is to guide the experience and cultivate your small group into a kind of teaching community. This will make it a place for members to process, question, and reflect—not receive more instruction.

Before your first meeting, make sure everyone in the group gets a copy of the study guide. This will keep everyone on the same page and help the process run more smoothly. If some group members are unable to purchase the guide, arrange it so that people can share the resource with other group members. Giving everyone access to all the material will position this study to be as rewarding an experience as possible. Everyone should feel free to write in his or her study guide and bring it to group every week.

SETTING UP THE GROUP

You will need to determine with your group how long you want to meet each week so you can plan your time accordingly. Generally, most groups like to meet for either ninety minutes or two hours, so you could use one of the following schedules:

Section	90 Minutes	120 Minutes
Welcome (members arrive and get settled)	10 minutes	15 minutes
Share (discuss one or more of the opening questions for the session)	15 minutes	20 minutes
Watch (watch the teaching material together and take notes)	25 minutes	25 minutes
Discuss (discuss the Bible study questions you selected ahead of time)	30 minutes	45 minutes
Respond / Pray (pray together as a group and dismiss)	10 minutes	15 minutes

As the group leader, you'll want to create an environment that encourages sharing and learning. A church sanctuary or formal classroom may not be as ideal as a living room, because those locations can feel formal and less intimate. No matter what setting you choose, provide enough comfortable seating for everyone, and, if possible, arrange the seats in a semicircle so everyone can see the video easily. This will make transition between the video and group conversation more efficient and natural.

Also, try to get to the meeting site early so you can greet participants as they arrive. Simple refreshments create a welcoming atmosphere and can be a wonderful addition to a group study evening. Try to take food and pet allergies into account to make your guests as comfortable as possible. You may also want to consider offering childcare to couples with children who want to attend. Finally, be sure your media technology is working properly. Managing these details up front will make the rest of your group experience flow smoothly and provide a welcoming space in which to engage the content of *Sacred Pathways*.

STARTING THE GROUP TIME

Once everyone has arrived, it's time to begin the group. Here are some simple tips that will help you make your group time healthy, enjoyable, and effective.

First, begin the meeting with a short prayer and remind the group members to put their phones on silent. This is a way to make sure you can all be present with one another and with God. Next, give each person a few minutes to respond to the questions in the "Talk About It" section. This won't require as much time in session one, but beginning in session two, people will need more time to share their insights from their personal studies. Usually, you won't answer the discussion questions yourself, but you should go first with the "Talk About It" questions, answering briefly and with a reasonable amount of transparency.

At the beginning of session one, make sure that you plan some extra time for the group members to complete the personal assessment (generally ten to fifteen minutes). Taking this assessment at the start of the study will help them to get a grasp on each of the different pathways and which one(s) they might gravitate toward and want to pursue. They will learn more about their particular pathway as they go through this study.

At the end of session one, invite the group members to complete the between-sessions personal studies for that week. Explain that you will be providing some time before the video teaching next week for anyone to share insights. Let them know sharing is optional, and it's no problem if they can't get to some of the between-sessions activities some weeks. It will still be beneficial for them to hear from the other participants and learn about what they discovered.

LEADING THE DISCUSSION TIME

Now that the group is engaged, it's time to watch the video and respond with some directed small-group discussion. Encourage all the group members to participate in the discussion, but make sure they know they don't have to do so. As the discussion progresses, you may want to follow up with comments such as, "Tell me more about that," or, "Why did you answer that way?" This will allow the group participants to deepen their reflections and invite meaningful sharing in a nonthreatening way.

Note that you have been given multiple questions to use in each session, and you do not have to use them all or even follow them in any order. Feel free to pick and choose questions based on either the needs of your group or how the conversation is flowing. Also, don't be afraid of silence. Offering a question and allowing up to thirty seconds of silence is okay. It allows people space to think about how they want to respond and also gives them time to do so.

As group leader, you are the boundary keeper for your group. Do not let anyone (yourself included) dominate the group time. Keep an eye out for group members who might be tempted to "attack" folks they disagree with or try to "fix" those having struggles. These kinds of behaviors can derail a group's momentum, so they need to be steered in a different direction. Model active listening and encourage everyone in your group to do the same. This will make your group time a safe space and create a positive community.

The group discussion leads to a closing time of individual reflection and prayer. Encourage the participants to take a few moments to review what they've learned during the session. This will help them cement the big ideas in their minds as you close. Conclude by praying together as a group.

GROUP DYNAMICS

Leading a group study can be a rewarding experience for you and your group members—but that doesn't mean there won't be challenges. Certain members may feel uncomfortable discussing topics that they consider personal and might be afraid of being called on. Some members might have disagreements on specific issues. To help prevent these scenarios, consider the following ground rules:

- If someone has a question that may seem off topic, suggest that it is discussed at another time, or ask the group if they are okay with addressing that topic.

- If someone asks a question you don't know the answer to, confess that you don't know and move on. If you feel comfortable, invite other group members to give their opinions or share their comments based on personal experience.

- If you feel like a couple of people are talking much more than others, direct questions to people who may not have shared yet. You could even ask the more dominating members to help draw out the quiet ones.

- When there is a disagreement, encourage the group members to process the matter in love. Invite members from opposing sides to evaluate their opinions and consider the ideas of the other members. Lead the group through Scripture that addresses the topic, and look for common ground.

When issues arise, encourage your group to follow these words from Scripture: "Love one another" (John 13:34); "If it is possible, as much as it depends on you, live peaceably with all men" (Romans 12:18); "Whatever things are true . . . noble . . . pure . . . lovely . . . if there is any virtue and if there is anything praiseworthy—meditate on these things" (Philippians 4:8); and, "Be swift to hear, slow to speak, slow to wrath" (James 1:19). This will make your group time more rewarding and beneficial for everyone who attends.

Thank you again for your willingness to lead your group. May God reward your efforts and dedication, equip you to guide your group in the weeks ahead, and make your time together in *Sacred Pathways* fruitful for his kingdom.

Also Available from Gary Thomas

If your spiritual walk is not what you'd like it to be, you can change that, starting here. *Sacred Pathways* will show you the route you were made to travel, marked by growth and filled with the riches of a close walk with God.

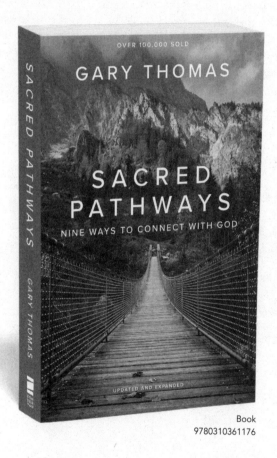

Book
9780310361176

Available now at your favorite bookstore.

Jesus Walked Away from Toxic People, and You Should Too

In this book and six-session video Bible study, bestselling author Gary Thomas draws on Jesus' example to show how the best course of action for us to take with toxic relationships is to walk away...or let the other person walk away. In the Gospels, when Jesus spoke a hard truth, sometimes the other person walked away or asked Jesus to leave—and he complied. Other times, people begged Jesus to stay, but he walked away so he could remain completely focused on the mission God had for him. We can, and should, do the same.

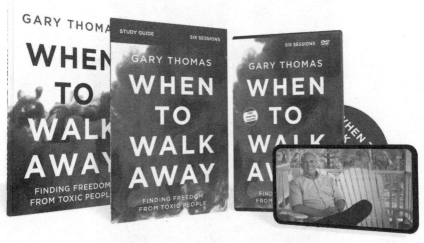

Book
9780310346760

Study Guide
9780310110248

DVD with FREE streaming
9780310110361

Available now at your favorite bookstore,
or streaming video on StudyGateway.com.

Breathe New Life into Your Marriage

Most married couples survive by gritting their teeth and holding on. However, as Gary Thomas reveals in this six-session video Bible study, couples can not only survive but actually thrive in marriage when they learn how to cherish one another. This simple practice of cherishing—noticing, appreciating, honoring, and encouraging one another—can reverse old patterns of "going through the motions" and bring hope and life into every marriage.

Book
9780310347262

DVD
9780310080749

Study Guide
9780310080732

Available now at your favorite bookstore,
or streaming video on StudyGateway.com.

Discover a Deeper Intimacy with God Through Your Marriage

In this six-session small group Bible study, writer and speaker Gary Thomas invites you to see how God can use marriage as a discipline and a motivation to reflect more of the character of Jesus.

Your marriage is much more than a union between you and your spouse; it is a spiritual discipline ideally suited to help you know God more fully and intimately. *Sacred Marriage* shifts the focus from marital enrichment to spiritual enrichment in ways that can help you love your mate more. Whether it is delightful or difficult, your marriage can become a doorway to a closer walk with God.

Book
9780310337379

Participant's Guide
9780310880660

DVD
9780310352266

Available now at your favorite bookstore, or streaming video on StudyGateway.com.

Parenting Is a School for Spiritual Formation—and Our Children Are Our Teachers

What if one of God's primary intentions for you as a parent isn't about successfully raising perfect children, but about you becoming more holy? In this book and six-session video group study, award-winning author Gary Thomas shows how God can transform lessons in raising children into opportunities to grow in the image of Christ. It will help you and your group look at parenting from a different perspective: as a method of spiritual formation expressly designed by God to shape your soul in ways you cannot imagine.

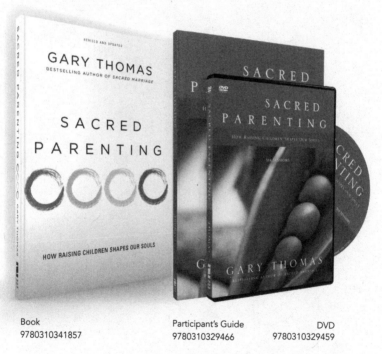

Book	Participant's Guide	DVD
9780310341857	9780310329466	9780310329459

Available now at your favorite bookstore,
or streaming video on StudyGateway.com.

Also Available from Gary Thomas

With all new material, 52 devotions explore the spiritual dynamics of parenting. These life-related devotions are creative, fresh, and encouraging, inspiring mothers and fathers to look at parenting from a different perspective—as a holy and high calling from God, and as an opportunity to grow spiritually as you strive to raise godly children. *Devotions for Sacred Parenting* helps you understand how God is parenting you as you parent your children.

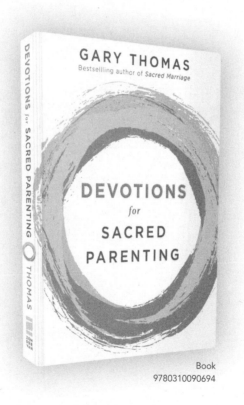

Book
9780310090694

Available now at your favorite bookstore.